HOW TO WRITE A STORY

SIMON CHESHIRE

Illustrated by
KATE PANKHURST

BLOOMSBURY
Activity Books

This colour edition of *How to Write a Story*
published 2015 by Bloomsbury Publishing Plc
50 Bedford Square, London, WC1B 3DP
www.bloomsbury.com

Bloomsbury is a registered trademark of Bloomsbury Publishing Plc

ISBN 978-1-4088-6657-3

Copyright © Bloomsbury Publishing Plc
Text © Simon Cheshire
Illustrations © Kate Pankhurst
Additional Illustrations © Shutterstock

A CIP record for this book is available from the British Library.

FSC
www.fsc.org

MIX
Paper from
responsible sources
FSC® C020056

Printed in China by Leo Paper Products, Heshan Guangdong
1 3 5 7 9 10 8 6 4 2

CONTENTS

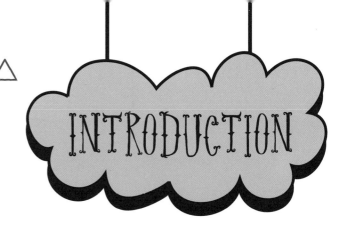

Welcome to the world of writing!

This book is designed to help you . . .

⭐ **Understand** how stories are put together

⭐ Switch on your brain cells and think up some **great ideas**

⭐ Write and present your work well (And also find out some **interesting facts** about writing and writers along the way!)

You can either work your way through the book from start to finish,

OR you can dive in wherever you like and hop back and forth. There are lots of activities to try, and plenty of helpful hints and tips scattered throughout.

So, what are you waiting for . . . ?

5

CHAPTER 1
WHAT YOU NEED

Your mission:
to master the amazing and mind-blowing art of... story-telling! Read on to find some hints and tips to help you on your way.

Your imagination

There are **many ways** stories can be told. Books, comic strips, films, TV shows, in songs, through dance, in paintings - the list goes on and on. People have been telling stories since the days of living in caves, shouting, '**ug**' and wearing fur dresses.

Stories aren't just words on a page, because as you read those words the story plays out in your head, *letting your imagination* run **wild.** So you, the reader, are an important part of the story's telling. The way you 'see' the story, in your imagination, is **entirely up to you**. The words may be the same for everyone, but nobody in the entire Universe can see that story exactly like you do in your imagination. Which means that, when you write a story, you're creating something **new and different** for every person who reads it.

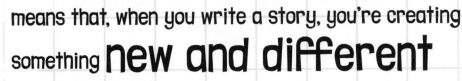

ACTIVITY

Try reading this and **not** picturing the scene in your head . . .

The grassy meadow

basked in the hazy sunshine of late afternoon. A gurgling river flowed gently through it. People sat, walked and played, enjoying the warm weather and the peaceful surroundings in their different ways. Trees, of all shapes and sizes, threw pools of shade across the grass. Insects flew among the wild flowers, and sparrows chirped in the hedgerows.

Not easy, is it?

Get together with a friend and read the previous page out loud. Everyone has one minute to sketch the scene in as much detail as possible - **no looking at each other's work!** Once the time is up, compare your sketches. They'll show the same basic scene, but you'll be amazed at how different they look.

Somewhere to put your work

Before you get stuck into your story you need to first decide **how** you're going to write it. Below are the two most commonly used forms authors use to write their stories, along with some **advantages** and **disadvantages** of each choice.

1 Pen and paper

The pen and paper has been a firm **favourite** of many authors for years. They're easy to carry around, you can use them **anywhere** and they're usually quite **cheap**. However it's not always easy to correct or change bits of your story and if you lose it then you don't have any other copies.

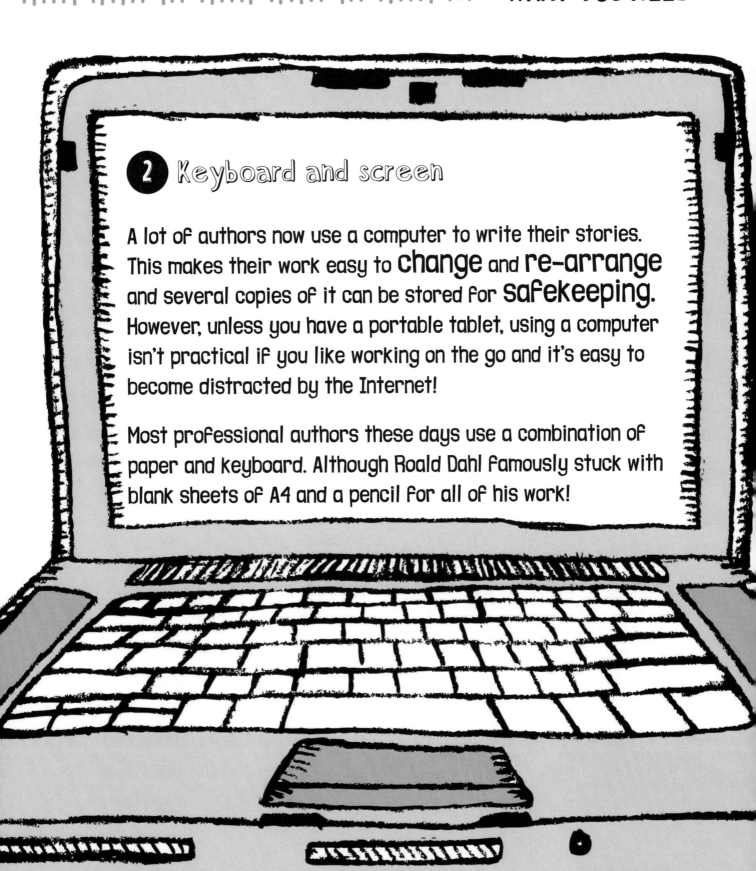

② Keyboard and screen

A lot of authors now use a computer to write their stories. This makes their work easy to **change** and **re-arrange** and several copies of it can be stored for **safekeeping**. However, unless you have a portable tablet, using a computer isn't practical if you like working on the go and it's easy to become distracted by the Internet!

Most professional authors these days use a combination of paper and keyboard. Although Roald Dahl famously stuck with blank sheets of A4 and a pencil for all of his work!

CHAPTER 2
PLANNING YOUR STORY

It's important to **plan your work** before you dive into it. Read on for some **ideas** to help plan your story.

How to plan

Planning is a **critical part** of any story. If your story is any longer than a few paragraphs, you're going to need to plan it out **carefully**. There are lots of ways to plan and here are two key examples that authors often use.

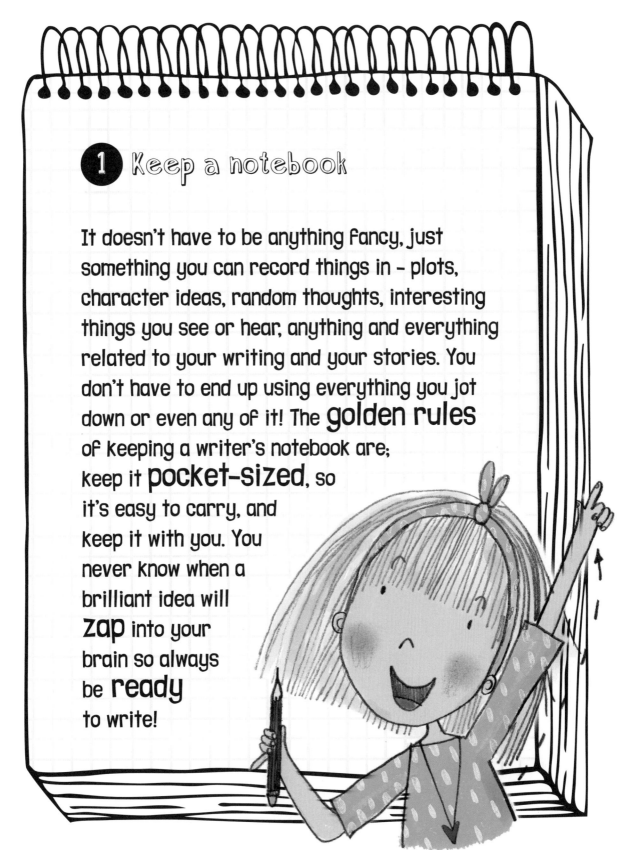

1 Keep a notebook

It doesn't have to be anything fancy, just something you can record things in – plots, character ideas, random thoughts, interesting things you see or hear, anything and everything related to your writing and your stories. You don't have to end up using everything you jot down or even any of it! The **golden rules** of keeping a writer's notebook are; keep it **pocket-sized**, so it's easy to carry, and keep it with you. You never know when a brilliant idea will **zap** into your brain so always be **ready** to write!

2 Bits of paper

By using the simple 'bits of paper' method you can jot down your thoughts and ideas **anywhere** and on **anything.**

You can then stick them to your planning 'area' (this could just be a bit of your bedroom wall) so that you gradually assemble an array of interesting or **useful snippets**. The good thing about this method is that you can add, remove, re-arrange and change stuff easily. And looking at all of your notes in one go can often **spark ideas** and connections you hadn't thought about before. The bad thing about this method is that bits and pieces can get lost if you're not careful!

Nearly all professional writers plan their stories carefully, but everyone approaches their **planning** in their own way. As you plan your stories, try different methods of **organising** your thoughts, and you'll soon discover what works best for you.

Brilliant beginnings, magnificent middles and amazing endings

The **plot** of your story isn't only a question of **what** happens, but also **why** it happens. As the writer of the story, it's up to you to make sure that when someone reads it, it's set out **clearly** and **logically**, from **start to finish**. Don't forget that your readers won't have gone through all the thinking and planning that you have – they know nothing about it!

When thinking about the overall structure of your story (how the plot unfolds) there's one thing you should always bear in mind: between the beginning and the end of the story,

- **How have things changed?**
- **How is life different for your characters?**
- **What has been gained?**
- **What has been lost?**

IT'S OFTEN USEFUL TO THINK ABOUT A PLOT BY SPLITTING IT INTO . . .

1 ...The Beginning

You need to **introduce your setting** and characters to your reader and show them around the world of your story. Is it dangerous or friendly? Nice or nasty? Who lives there? How are the events of your story going to be set up?

ACTIVITY

Pick six fiction books from a shelf at random (your school or classroom library might be a good place for this). Read the first chapter of each book. Think about how the world of the story is introduced to the reader – is it through **descriptions? or action? or both?**

PLANNING YOUR STORY

2 . . .The Middle

This is the 'meat' of your plot, the fuel in your story's boiler! The story gathers pace and excitement, events happen. What problems and difficulties must your hero meet? Who helps and who hinders your hero? And why?

ACTIVITY

List ten **twists**, or **complications**, which you could add to a plot to increase the **action** or make things more challenging for your characters. For example, a friend turns out to have been an enemy all along or our heroes discover that they've been looking at the treasure map upside down and they're miles from the correct spot.

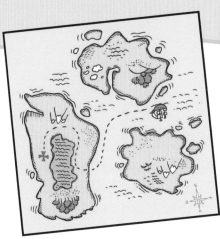

24

 7

 8

 9

 10

3 ... The End

This is the section where problems and difficulties are **overcome** (or not, as the case may be!). The events of the story are **concluded**. How are things **resolved**? Does your hero win or lose? At the end, how has the world of your story, and the characters in it, been affected?

ACTIVITY

Pick a favourite or familiar story. Think carefully about the **events** in the story, and imagine how things might have **ended differently**. For instance, Little Red Riding Hood might have ended with the wolf eating everyone, and getting a terrible stomach ache. Or Cinderella might have ended with one of the ugly sisters fitting into the glass slipper, and the prince having to marry her instead! Can you think of any other familiar stories that you could change the ending to?

Characters

Creating **interesting characters** to put in your story isn't easy. Below are some useful tips to help you plan them.

1 Characters must fit comfortably into your story

For example, a story about a family moving house might include some children, a parent or two, a pet cat, and perhaps some removal men, but it probably shouldn't include a slobbering alien monster. If it did, that would most likely be a story about the monster and not about the family who are moving house.

ACTIVITY

Write a short list of characters who might suit . . .

A WESTERN

Try drawing them if it helps. Can you write a description of them too?

31

A SPACE ADVENTURE

A LOVE STORY

A SPY STORY

2 Your main characters must have enough to do

Some characters might only appear briefly, but you'll certainly have characters who feature in many or all parts of the story. These main characters all need to play a **proper role.**

For example, if you wrote a story about a spy called Agent X and his trusty assistant Digby, then you should make sure Digby doesn't simply follow Agent X around and stand back while Agent X does all the hero stuff. Digby needs to **speak up**, and **take action** here and there, otherwise why is he in the story at all?

3 Characters should be distinct from each other

As your story unfolds, your readers need to be able to tell **one character from another** easily, otherwise things can become confusing. Some good ways to make characters **stand out** from each other might be . . .

. . . different ways of talking.
One character might talk at great length instead of getting to the point, while another just shrugs and says 'yeah' or 'nahh.' One character might use a particular phrase, or speak in a particular tone of voice.

. . . different behaviour. For example, one character could have a slow walk, while another scurries along. Or you could give a character a habit such as tapping their fingers, or sneezing a lot.

. . . different looks. If they look too similar, it's difficult for your readers to imagine them. If you have a story with three main characters you could make them distinct by having one of them tall with dark hair, one short with fair hair, and one with totally crazy hair and big feet. You could give a character something very specific that they always wear, or a distinctive pair of glasses, or even . . . a scar!

4 Before you start a story, think about various aspects of a character

If you know what your character is like, as a person, it helps you write about them in a **clear** and **interesting** way.

ACTIVITY

Think of a character, then make a list describing . . .

☆ How they look and dress

☆ How they speak and behave

☆ What they like to eat

☆ What hobbies or interests they have

☆ Any other aspect of them that comes to mind, no matter how odd or obscure, from when they have a bath to what they got for Christmas when they were six!

You certainly don't need to include all (or any) of this sort of information in your story, but the **clearer** a character is in your mind, the **better** you'll be able to write about them.

5 You should always name your characters carefully

A name alone can conjure up a powerful impression of what a character is like.

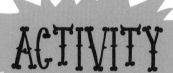

ACTIVITY

Think carefully about a character called **Baron Laserblast.** What's he like? How does he talk? Where does he live? How does he fill his day? When you've thought up plenty of details about him, try doing exactly the same thing, for a character named **Violet Sweetly.** You should end up with two very different characters! Where did you get all that information about them? Just their names!

Baron Laserblast

_____
_____
_____
_____
_____
_____
_____
_____
_____
_____
_____

Violet Sweetly

_____
_____
_____
_____
_____
_____
_____
_____
_____
_____
_____

Think of a character name and then draw the character to go with that name . . .

Now swap the order and draw a character first, and then think up a name that might suit them!

ACTIVITY

Here are two characters - try thinking up names (and any other details you like) that would fit them.

CHARACTER NO.1

CHARACTER NO.2

43

CHARACTER NO.1

CHARACTER NO.2

6 You need to know why your characters do this or that

A **good character** always has good reasons for their actions. For example, if you're writing a story in which aliens invade Earth, you might tell your readers that they're doing it just because they're nasty and evil. However, it would be much more effective to give the aliens more **interesting motives**. Perhaps their own planet has blown up, and they need a new home? Perhaps they're only doing it to stop something worse happening?

Ask yourself: what are these characters aiming to achieve and why? Knowing what your characters want is always a help when you're writing about them. For example, if your villain is trying to blow up the Moon, make sure he's not simply doing it to be evil. Perhaps his Mum is secretly a werewolf, and he wants to destroy the Moon so that she doesn't start howling and chewing up the carpet every few weeks.

7 **Don't be afraid to use bits and pieces of real-life people you know in your characters**

No, not arms, legs and eyeballs! **Things they do, things they say,** the way they wear a favourite coat, that sort of stuff. There can't be a single fiction writer in the world who hasn't taken snippets of people they've met and weaved them into their stories!

Who do you want to write about? Think of the most interesting person you know and get writing!

Who says what?

Who are the most **important characters** in your story?
Is one character more central to the story than all the others?
Who is your story mainly 'about'? It's important to plan all of
these details in advance so you don't get confused in the middle
of your story.

1 Point of view

As you plan and write your story, you need to consider from
whose point of view you're telling it. From the **perspective**
of which character (or characters) are we going to see the
action? Whose **experience** do you want to write about? For
example, if your story is about a bank robbery, we the readers
could 'witness' the crime from the point of view of . . .

☆ The thief

☆ An employee at the bank

☆ A passer-by

☆ The police officer who chases the crook

☆ Or someone else entirely!

Some stories are told from several **points of view.** For instance, you might have alternate chapters told in the voices of two different characters on two sides of the same story, or there might be separate sections of the plot, which highlight the **actions** of particular characters.

There's nothing wrong with telling your story from different points of view, but be careful not to switch between points of view too much or include too many points of view, which can be confusing for your readers.

2 Narrative 'mode'

First person narrative tells the story from a personal point of view, "I got up last Saturday, and I went to the shops".

Third person narrative tells the story from the writer's point of view, "Jack got up last Saturday, and he went to the shops".
You can use either first or third person narration, but there are a couple of points to bear in mind:

⭐ **First person narrative** is best for telling stories in which there is one main character, and/or in which the story involves sharing the main character's thoughts or feelings a lot. It's a very good way to get the reader inside the character's head in order to understand the character's actions and reactions.

⭐ **Third person narrative** is best for telling stories which have lots of characters, or where the story needs to change location or point of view regularly. It's good for describing action and more complicated plots, because you can more easily hop from scene to scene, or from time to time, or tell the reader what's happening in more than one way.

What's **second person narrative?**
It's very rarely used to tell stories, because it sounds a bit strange - "You got up last Saturday, and you went to the shops".

ACTIVITY

Try writing a one-page story using first person narrative, then retell the whole thing using third person narrative. What changes in the way each version is told?

What type of story are you telling?

It's important that your story has a **clear tone** and that the way you tell it is the same from start to finish. There's nothing wrong with mixing up **laughs, scares, sad bits** and **action** all in the same story – in fact, some of the best stories do exactly that – however, the style in which your story is told needs to be **consistent** all the way through.

For example, if you were writing a funny story, you need to make sure that **funny bits** turn up regularly. It's no good having a hilarious, side-splitting first chapter and then no laughs at all in the rest of the story. It's fine to include a few **jokes** in a horror story, or a few **tense moments** in a comedy, but these must be used lightly and sparingly. Here are a couple of quick, useful ways to create the right **atmosphere.**

1 Mis-match of character and setting

Some **comedy**, especially on TV and in films, is based around this idea. Remember how important it is to choose characters who fit neatly into your story? One way of writing comedy is to **choose a character who doesn't!**

How did you get here?

ACTIVITY

Try thinking up some mis-matched characters who might raise some laughs in . . .

☆ A beauty salon
☆ A space ship
☆ Your classroom at school

For example, in a Wild West town, mis-matched characters might be a Sheriff and a giant troll, or a gunslinger and a footballer.

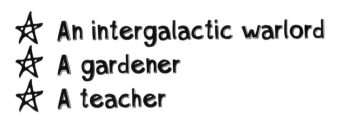ACTIVITY

Now try placing the following characters into settings where they'd create laughs instead of drama . . .

★ An intergalactic warlord
★ A gardener
★ A teacher

For example, someone zooming about on a motorbike wouldn't fit into a classroom when the pupils are trying to get some work done.

② Dramatic irony

Both comedy and horror stories can use what's called **dramatic irony.** In fact, lots of different types of story can use this! Dramatic irony is a situation in which we, the readers or the audience, know something that the characters in the story don't.

An example scene of dramatic irony in a horror story might be:

Fred comes home, not realising that there's a mad axe-wielding murderer in the kitchen. We know the murderer's there, sharpening his axe, but Fred goes about the house, having no idea what danger he's in. Finally, he goes to make a cup of tea and arrrgghhhh!

An example scene of dramatic irony in a funny story might be:

Fred comes home, not realising that the dripping tap in the kitchen has now become a gushing fountain which is starting to fill the room with water. We know it's gushing, he doesn't. He potters about, going nowhere near the kitchen. Then, finally, he opens the kitchen door, and a giant wall of water whooshes out.

Settings

Choosing **where** and **when** your story takes place might seem simple at first, but you need to ensure that your setting and your story don't conflict with each other. For example, if a vital part of your plot involves your hero searching online for information, you obviously can't set your story in Victorian times (no Internet)!

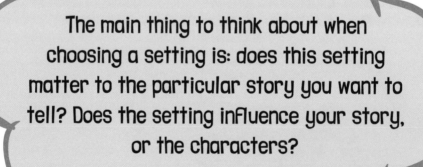

The main thing to think about when choosing a setting is: does this setting matter to the particular story you want to tell? Does the setting influence your story, or the characters?

 For each of these brief plot ideas, try to think of several different settings into which they might fit:

⭐ Charlie discovers that his best friend, Paul, has **stolen** something. Nobody else knows about it. Then Charlie finds himself **accused** of the crime!

SETTING 1 :

SETTING 2 :

SETTING 3 :

SETTING 4 :

SETTING 5 :

SETTING 6 :

⭐ Fred tells Sarah he's an **expert** on something. He isn't. He **lied** to impress her. Then Sarah arranges for Fred to give a talk on the subject.

SETTING 1 :

SETTING 2 :

SETTING 3 :

SETTING 4 :

SETTING 5 :

SETTING 6 :

⭐ Alice makes a **cake** for Isobel. Isobel thinks it tastes **disgusting**, but she says she likes it. She doesn't want to hurt Alice's **feelings**. Alice is so pleased, she makes Isobel two more cakes!

SETTING 1 : _____

SETTING 2 : _____

SETTING 3 : _____

SETTING 4 : _____

SETTING 5 : _____

SETTING 6 : _____

For each setting that you think of, ask yourself these questions about how the setting affects the story:

- Are there any **events** that could/ should/ can't happen because of this setting?

- Are there ways in which the characters might **act** or **behave** differently in this setting?

- Does this setting influence the way the story **ends**?

Whatever setting you choose
for your story, don't forget to use plenty
of **descriptive words** when you write about it.
For example, instead of saying, "The old house was
dark and shabby" you could add descriptive details
to make it more interesting: "The house was a dark
shadow of what it had once been, a sad and empty
shell with cracked windows and a peeling front
door." A story's setting should be every bit
as **vivid** and **memorable**
as its characters or plot!

Story mountains

It's often useful, when you're **planning** the **plot** of your story, to keep in mind a simple visual map to help you think about organising things **effectively**. The most commonly used **visual map** is called a **story mountain** but they are just one of many easy-to-use tools to help you structure your story's plot. Below is an example of how to use one.

The Problem
Something has gone wrong! Or perhaps there is a mystery that needs to be solved. Have there been any disagreements?

The Build-Up
How can you build up excitement in your story? What has happened? Are there any clues? What has been said?

The Resolution
How is the problem going to be solved? How can you make your characters happy again?

The Beginning
Introduce your main characters and describe the setting.

The Ending
Is it a happy ending? Have your characters learned a lesson? Have any of your characters developed?

Create your own **story mountain.**

CHAPTER 3
WRITING YOUR STORY

You've discovered tips on planning your story and now it's time to **get writing!** Read on to uncover some **inspirational ideas** on how to get started!

The words

We all know what 'parts of speech' are, right? If you do, then this is a reminder of how **important** it is to know them. If you don't, then this is the perfect way to get up to speed, and **fast!**

There are **eight** basic parts of speech, or types of word.
They are:

1 NOUNS: Words for things or people

For example, house, train, John, cup, dog, Charlotte, teacher.

2 VERBS: Words for doing or being

For example, jump, be, can, have, run, belch, talk, climb.

3 ADJECTIVES: Words which describe a noun

For example, big, small, red, furry, fierce,
boring, exciting, good, bad, cold.

4 ADVERBS: Words which describe something other than a noun (normally a verb)

For example, quickly, slowly, badly, warmly, often, very, unfortunately.

5 PRONOUNS: A word used in place of a noun

For example, he, she, we, it, his.

We need pronouns to avoid repeating nouns, so that we can say, "The bear was hungry and it ate my leg" instead of, "The bear was hungry and the bear ate my leg".

"I'll have the leg"

6 PREPOSITIONS: Words that link nouns (or pronouns) to other words

For example, to, at, after, above, with, from.
They tell us how one thing is related to another, "We played on the beach", "John went to school", "Mary left the party before the robot".

7 CONJUNCTIONS: Words that stick bits of sentences together

For example but, and, because, since, while, when.
So we can say, "I washed my socks and left the house" instead of "I washed my socks. I left the house".

8 INTERJECTIONS: 'Outburst' words that express emotions or exclamations

For example, Ow! Hi! Wow! Oh! Ah! However, these don't include words like bang, zap or kapow. Words like these, which imitate a noise, are called **onomatopoeia.**

ACTIVITY

Try listing two or three examples of each eight types of word from the pages before – and no, you can't use the ones already mentioned!

1 NOUNS

2 VERBS

3 ADJECTIVES

4 ADVERBS

70

5 PRONOUNS

6 PREPOSITIONS

7 CONJUNCTIONS

8 INTERJECTIONS

ARTICLES

There's also a special sort of adjective called an 'article.' **Articles** are words which accompany nouns. In English, we use **'indefinite articles'**, namely 'a' and 'an' (a boat, an apple) and we have one **'definite article'**, namely 'the' (the goat, the tree, the alien).

As well as articles, there are loads of other things to discover about **word usage** and how words and sentences are put together. This is called **'grammar'**. However, we could easily fill up the rest of this book with this information, and it can all get **v-e-r-y** complicated. As long as you're familiar with the eight basic parts of speech, you shouldn't go too far wrong!

Try to identify and list different parts of speech in each of these sentences – it's harder than it looks!

1

The monster ran to the toilet, but he tripped and hit his nose.

2

Jake looked into the box and saw his dusty old teddy bear.

3

When she arrives, tell her the pool is full of green jelly.

Structure

Proper paragraphs!

Correct punctuation!

Well-formed sentences!

Do they really matter?

Of course they do!

Good writing isn't just about choosing the right words, it's about **organising** them **properly.** This will help your readers to **understand** your story, so it's very important that you **express** yourself clearly. Read on for some key ideas to help organise your story.

1 Paragraphs

Paragraphs are an excellent **organising** tool. They help you layout your story **clearly** for your reader.

There are no firm rules about how to **structure** your paragraphs. Some people say that paragraphs should always be at least two or three sentences long. Some people don't. At the end of the day, it's up to you – the important thing is that each paragraph is there for a **reason**, not just to break up the words or look pretty on the page.

Compare paragraphs in, for example, a **newspaper** and a **novel** for grown-ups. You'll find they look very different.

Now try writing some paragraphs of your own.

A lot of **modern writers** use short, single-sentence paragraphs to create a **dramatic** effect.
For example . . .

Dick Deadly the private eye crept closer to the door of his office. The lights were on inside. He was sure he'd turned them off when he left. As long as the bag of money was still on his desk, all was well. If not, he was in big trouble.

Slowly, he gripped the door handle. He leant against the door, preparing to burst in. He took a long, deep breath, then flung the door open.

The money was gone.

This is a good way to **grab** your reader's **attention**. However, only use this trick now and again. If you use it too much, it stops being dramatic and starts looking a bit silly.

② Punctuation

Full stops, commas, question marks and all the other dots, dashes and squiggles which make up English punctuation are even more important than paragraphs in helping to organise words. Without correct punctuation, English is just gibberish.

Try adding in punctuation to the following passage so the story makes sense. If you find it easier, use the space provided to rewrite the passage with all of the correct punctuation in place.

the other day my friend amy said steve why have you got that strange hat on thats not a hat thats my new haircut I said I couldnt believe she d mistaken my very expensive hairdo for a hat later on I met my other friend mike whats that terrible wig youre wearing he said wig that's not a wig thats my actual hair mike I said I wasnt having a very good day

Presenting your work

If you present your story in a confusing or unattractive way, your readers will find it hard to get through it, no matter how good it is! Below are some things to think about:

1 Paragraphs

When writing stories, should you mark **new paragraphs** using a line space, or an indent? One thing's definite: stories normally look **h-o-r-r-i-b-l-e** with line spaced paragraphs, especially where you've got a couple of characters having a conversation. There's a simple rule: for fiction, indents. For non-fiction, line spaces.

2 Margins

Take care with **margins**, the spaces around your text to the left and right, top and bottom. If they're too small, your page will look like it's overflowing with words. Too large, and your page will look strangely empty.

3 Titles and headings

It's fine to put your story's title or chapter headings in **BIG** or **bold letters**, but avoid doing it in the text of the story itself. It will distract your reader's eye!

4 Fiddly bits

When typing a story, be careful when using *italics*, <u>underlined</u> or **bold** letters. These can be used to **emphasise**, or **pick out**, particular words. In non-fiction, they're a great way to draw attention to the important bits but in fiction they're hardly ever needed. This book is an example of a non-fiction book.

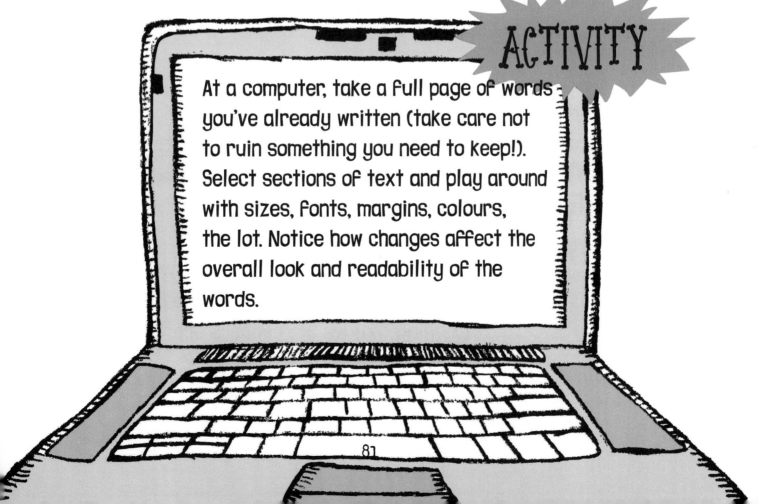

ACTIVITY

At a computer, take a full page of words you've already written (take care not to ruin something you need to keep!). Select sections of text and play around with sizes, fonts, margins, colours, the lot. Notice how changes affect the overall look and readability of the words.

Speech and tenses

It's important to have a clear idea of how things are going to be said in your text and also whether or not they're going to happen in the **past** or in the **present**. Read on to find out more.

1 Direct and reported speech

Here are two ways of saying the same thing:

> George told Auntie Kate that he was sorry for kicking the ball through her window. Auntie Kate replied that he could pay for the repair and that she was shocked at his behaviour.

> "I'm really sorry," said George.
> "You can jolly well pay for that window, young man!" cried Auntie Kate. "I'm very disappointed in you! What dreadful behaviour!"

The first uses **'reported speech'**, meaning that we the readers are told about something being said. The second uses **'direct speech'**, meaning that we the readers are told what was said.

It's often better to use **direct speech** in stories if you can. It's **livelier,** better for showing the character of the person who's speaking, and it usually feels **more natural.** **Reported speech** is very useful if you want to **summarise** something, without having to repeat it.

For example, if Chapter Two of your story is a **dramatic** description of how George climbs Mount Everest, then when you get to Chapter Three and George is back home, you can say "George told his Auntie Kate all about his adventure on the mountain", instead of having to give George an enormous speech beginning "Well, we set off . . ." which just repeats the action of the previous chapter.

ACTIVITY

Find some examples of direct and reported speech.

Hint: news reports are good for this.

2 Using tenses

Stories can be told in either the **Past Tense** or the **Present Tense**. The important thing is not to mix your tenses! Below are some examples.

Past Tense:

The time for the final race had arrived. The whistle blew. All four runners shot off the starting line. The crowd cheered, urging the athletes on. For many metres, they were neck and neck, their feet pounding the track. Then Jack, his face strained with effort, began to pull ahead.

Present Tense:

It's time for the final race. The whistle blows. All four runners shoot off the starting line. The crowd cheers, urging the athletes on. For many metres, they're neck and neck, their feet are pounding the track. Then Jack, his face straining with effort, begins to pull ahead.

Choose a couple of paragraphs from a book, newspaper or website. Try rewriting them in a different tense. Then rewrite them in another tense!

Kick-start your story!

Here are some **sentences** you could use to **kick-start** your story. You could make them the first words of the story, or part of the first paragraph. Adapt them to suit your own ideas, or simply use them as a way of revving up your **imagination!**

★ "You see that boy over there?" she said. "You'll never guess what he told me."

★ It was the day the school exploded.

★ Higher and higher we climbed, until the ground vanished beneath the clouds.

★ The letter I received that morning was unlike any I'd ever read before.

★ "Do you believe in monsters?" said the strange, booming voice.

★ School kids don't chase crooks. At least, that's what Jim thought.

★ Despite the storm, the tall ship sailed into the harbour.

★ As soon as the plane taxied onto the runway, I realised what I'd forgotten.

★ Katie found the poor creature in the garden, and took it indoors out of the cold.

★ There was a circular gap in the dust, showing where it had been taken.

★ He had no choice. It had to be done.

★ "Oh no, not again," he cried.

★ The village had nestled peacefully in the valley until the strangers came.

★ I always like to start my day with a song.

★ At first, the instruction manual seemed quite simple.

★ A slow, terrible panic began to grip my throat.

★ He heard a weird noise, and assumed at first that it was just the cat.

★ It started well. It ended badly.

★ This was definitely the oddest school she'd ever seen.

★ He was absolutely sure that both his feet had changed size since lunchtime.

ACTIVITY

Why not try . . .
★ Writing a story which uses two or more of these kick-starter sentences.

☆ Now try writing a story which begins with one kick-starter sentence, and ends with another.

Brain freeze

Have you ever found yourself staring at a blank piece of paper and not knowing what to write about? Don't worry – you're not alone. Every writer, even the most successful, experiences times when they just can't get their minds into gear!

Here are a few ideas to help get your creativity up to top speed again.

1 Take action

Go for a brisk walk to blow the dust off your brain or pop down to the corner shop for a pint of milk. You could even do the washing up if you're feeling brave enough. Moving your limbs around is often a good way to get your thoughts moving too. Why? It's a bit of a mystery, to be honest. But it works!

2 Write something else

If you're stuck for story ideas, take a little time out and write a few paragraphs on any other subject you happen to think of – anything at all! Sometimes, thinking about a totally different topic for a while can be very refreshing.

ACTIVITY

Use this space to write about anything that's not part of your story. If you're stuck, try using these ideas . . .

My Favourite Movie

The Greatest Cake I Ever Ate

What To Do If The Martians Invade

3 Act out a character

Another **good trick** is to do a bit of acting. Become a fictional character for half an hour. Any character you like. Do things the way they'd do it, speak the way they'd speak. You'd be amazed at how new ideas can pop into your head, not just about characters but about plots and other stuff too!

Ahem, a word of warning: this is probably best done when you're on your own, unless you don't mind other people giving you funny looks. (Or maybe they could join in!)

ACTIVITY

Try acting out the following . . .

☆ A character from the last book you read
☆ A character based on one of your teachers
☆ A character based on someone on TV

4 Try some 'free writing'

Get a pen and paper and something to time yourself. Give yourself ten minutes and from the second that ten minutes starts, you must write **non-stop!** You can write anything that comes into your head, no matter how **crazy** or **random** but your pen must barely leave the paper! You're not allowed to stop, not for anything at all, until the ten minutes is up. What you're left with is probably a page of totally useless weirdness, but the insides of your mind have now had a good clean-out!

5 Take a break

If all else fails, simply leave your story for a while. Just a day or two may be enough. In the meantime, think about something completely different. Come back to your story after some time away from it, and you'll probably see it in a whole new light.

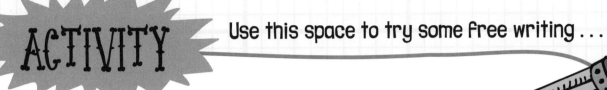

ACTIVITY

Use this space to try some free writing . . .

Can any of the stuff you've written be used to create a good story?

Improving your writing

Here's a selection of **ideas, activities, exercises and suggestions** for things to do which will expand your writing experience and boost your literary skills.

1 Tackle an unfamiliar genre

If you like writing **ghost stories**, try writing a story about a pony instead. If you like stories about **history**, try one set in the far **future**. Writing something well outside your comfort zone is a great way to get a **fresh view** of the whole writing process.

2 Co-operate on a story

Write a story **with a friend**. One of you could write the first half, and the other the second half. Or one of you could plan out the **plot** and the **characters**, and the other could write the **story**.

3 Write a 'chapter chain'

One person writes the first chapter of a story, then hands it on to someone else, who writes the next chapter, and so on. You could alternate between two or three writers, or involve all your friends. You could agree on a **subject** before you begin, or you could **write 'blind'**, so that each new writer has no idea what's coming up. Chapter chains often produce strange but **very entertaining** results!

4 Change a familiar story

Take any well-known story, traditional **folktales** or **fairy tales** work well for this, and retell it from the beginning in your own way. The only rule is that your version must be as different from the original as you can make it!

5 Write from real life

Take a look at the **people** and **events** currently in the news, either **online**, on **TV** or in **newspapers**. Imagine yourself in those situations. You could write a story, or perhaps a **fictional diary**, either from the point of view of someone in the news, or as if you yourself were there.

6 Write to order

Tell a story based on **suggestions**. Ask three people, separately, to suggest a **character**. They can give you as much or as little detail as they like. Ask a fourth person to suggest a **setting**. The school canteen, a building site, a cave on Mars, anything at all. Now you must write a story using that setting and all three characters. You're not allowed to change them, you must use the suggestions you've been given. What happens? Who's the hero? Is there a villain? This is quite a tricky exercise!

Story starters

Here are some additional ideas for getting your stories under way.

What if . . .

⭐ You woke up two hours late for school?

⭐ A giant earthworm came burrowing up through the school playing field?

⭐ You found out your best friend was doing something evil?

⭐ You discovered you're not a human being after all?

⭐ That fly on the wall was watching you?

⭐ The world's supply of oil ran out tomorrow?

⭐ A troll started living in your fridge?

☆ Your home was destroyed by a flood or a hurricane?

☆ Everyone vanished except you and your worst enemy?

☆ You found a bag full of money in the street?

☆ Nobody remembered your birthday?

☆ You won a competition to become Prime Minister?

☆ You could hear what other people were thinking?

☆ A notorious crook moved in next door?

☆ You lost your most precious possession?

☆ You won a lifetime supply of chocolate?

If all else fails, you could try . . .

The Randomiser!

Pick something at random from **column 1**, then pick something at random from **column 2** and then pick something at random from **column 3**! Ta-daa! You've got a story starter!

PARP!

A teeny tiny goat makes a smell

eat healthy

hot dog

A hungry alien goes to school

COLUMN 1	COLUMN 2	COLUMN 3
My favourite	friend	goes to the dentist
A scary	teacher	wins the lottery
The world's best	goat	zooms into space
A teeny tiny	girl	makes a smell
Europe's best-dressed	baby	goes to school
The world's worst	car	goes on TV
A really smelly	boy	tries ballroom dancing
Britain's noisiest	inventor	has a brilliant idea
My all-time top	swarm of insects	fights crime
A cruel	school bully	explores a mysterious cave
A hilariously funny	shop keeper	has a picnic in the park
A bright blue	parent	bakes a cake
A musical	tree	finds a lost city
A terribly boring	alien	travels through time
The UK's brainiest	aunt	is really a spy
A gigantic	leopard	builds a house
History's most terrifying	teddy bear	visits a theme park
An angry	monster	becomes a superhero
A hungry	dog	goes to sea

CHAPTER 4
TAKING IT FURTHER

The following chapter takes a closer look at some of the topics mentioned so far as well as looking at a few other forms of writing.

More on structure

We've looked at the basic parts of structure but below is a look at a few more nuggets of information that might help with your story writing.

Some facts about punctuation

✭ Brackets like this ( ) are called parentheses.

✭ A line of three dots like this . . . is called an ellipsis, and is used either to indicate a pause, a missing word, or to indicate that a thought is to be continued or remains unfinished. For example, "When he went to the zoo, he fell in a big pile of zebra's . . ." or "What happened to the spaceship after it vanished is anyone's guess . . ."

✭ A symbol like this &, can stand in for the word 'and', is called an ampersand. It first appeared in Roman times, when the letters 'e' and 't' would sometimes get written squashed up together.

✭ Exclamation marks like this ! used to be put at the end of every sentence in American comic books in the 1940s and '50s, because full stops often got lost when they were printed. An exclamation mark was the only way to clearly mark the end of a sentence.

✭ It's thought that the question mark ? may have evolved from placing the letter 'q' (for 'question') at the end of a sentence.

Sentence construction

Here are some ideas relating to sentence **construction** and writing **style**. There are lots of others, but these are some of the most common:

✭ **A simile** (pronounced sim-ee-lee) is a comparison, normally using the words 'like' or 'as'. For example, "She's as graceful as a gazelle" or, "The lights twinkled like stars".

✭ **A metaphor** is rather like a simile, but compares two things by saying they're the same. For example: "My heart is broken" - it's not literally broken, the 'being broken' bit is a metaphor for feeling sad.

ACTIVITY

Try coming up with your own **similes** and **metaphors**...

✭ An **allegory** is a bit like a metaphor, but it's an entire story in which characters or events are used as a **secret** way to talk about something else. For instance, you could write a story about a boy who flies to the Moon and meets some friendly aliens; this story might be an '**undercover**' way of talking about going to a new school and meeting new friends, because the boy's worries and feelings might be similar in both situations.

Now try coming up with your own **allegory**...

★ A **parody** is a story which **pokes fun** at something by **imitating** it in a **funny** way. For example, you might change *Alice In Wonderland* by writing a story about a girl who falls down a drain and meets someone called the Mad Natter who talks gobbledegook all the time.

Think of some titles for **parodies** of well-known books, films or TV series...

✮ **Irony** is the **dramatic** or **humorous** linking of **opposites**. It would be ironic if, for example, someone scared of leaving home in case he got eaten by an escaped lion then got eaten by a lion let loose in his own house. Or, if you spent all day waiting to see a rare butterfly, then missed it because you'd gone to the toilet for two minutes.

✮ A **cliché** (pronounced clee-shay) is a word or phrase that's used so much it becomes the most **obvious** or **dull** way to say something. Perhaps the most glaring clichés are "Once upon a time" and "They all lived happily ever after". Try and avoid these by finding a more original way to say it instead.

✮ A **hyperbole** (pronounced high-per-boll-ee) is a wild **exaggeration**, deliberately used to make a point. For example, "I've got a tonne of homework." Hyperboles can also be similes, as in "his legs are like matchsticks".

2 3 6

How many stories can there possibly be?

4

1

> Sometimes, different stories – about different subjects and different characters – can still have things in common. They might contain similar ideas, themes, or plots.

1 2

4

5

Raw ingredients

It's often said that the **raw ingredient** of any story is **change**. In other words, when you examine stories under a microscope, to see what makes them tick, they're all about stuff that happens. For instance, a princess fights a dragon, or a noisy new family move in next door. These are **events**, and events are the basic building blocks of stories. They could be big events, like a war, or teeny tiny events, like a pencil falling off a desk, but they all involve things going on.

Various writers, over the years, have boiled stories down to their **simplest forms**, and decided that there are only seven basic plots in the whole of fiction. As you might expect, there's plenty of disagreement over what those seven plots actually are. Read on for one possible version of them:

1 Quests

Any story involving a **long** and **hazardous journey**, in order to reach a valuable **prize** of some kind.

Examples include the ancient legend of *Jason and the Golden Fleece*, or Jules Verne's story *Around The World in Eighty Days*.

2 Rags To Riches

An ordinary or **lowly person** finds a better life (either literally, as in becoming **rich**, or metaphorically, as in finding **happiness**).

Examples include the story of *Cinderella*, or Charles Dickens's *David Copperfield*.

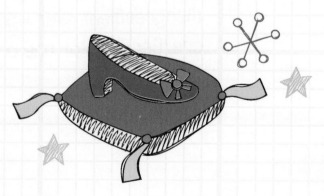

3 Defeat The Monster!

Our **hero** confronts a beast of some sort, either an actual **monster**, or perhaps simply something monstrous like an army of enemies or an **evil organisation**. Against all odds, the monster is defeated, and our hero often wins some sort of reward for their bravery. Examples include the story of *Jack and the Beanstalk*, or Bram Stoker's vampire novel *Dracula*.

4 Far, Far Away

Some unexpected event hurls our hero out of their familiar surroundings, and lands them in a **strange new world**.
Examples include Lewis Carroll's *Alice in Wonderland*, or H.G.Wells's science fiction tale *The Time Machine*.

5 Comedy

This doesn't necessarily mean a funny story, as such, but simply one in which a series of **complications** (sometimes romantic) end happily for all the characters.

Examples include most situation comedies on TV or the novels of *Jane Austen.*

6 Tragedy

The **opposite** of comedy - things end badly all round! Our hero, sometimes a person of wealth or importance, meets a series of **problems** or tough decisions. By making **bad choices**, they bring about their own **downfall.**

Examples include Shakespeare's characters Macbeth, Othello, Hamlet, and King Lear.

7 Caught In The Web

Our hero meets some form of evil power which traps them. They must show great courage, or change their ways somehow, before they can be released.

Examples include the story of *Sleeping Beauty,* and Charles Dickens's *A Christmas Carol.*

Think up some more examples of each story type.

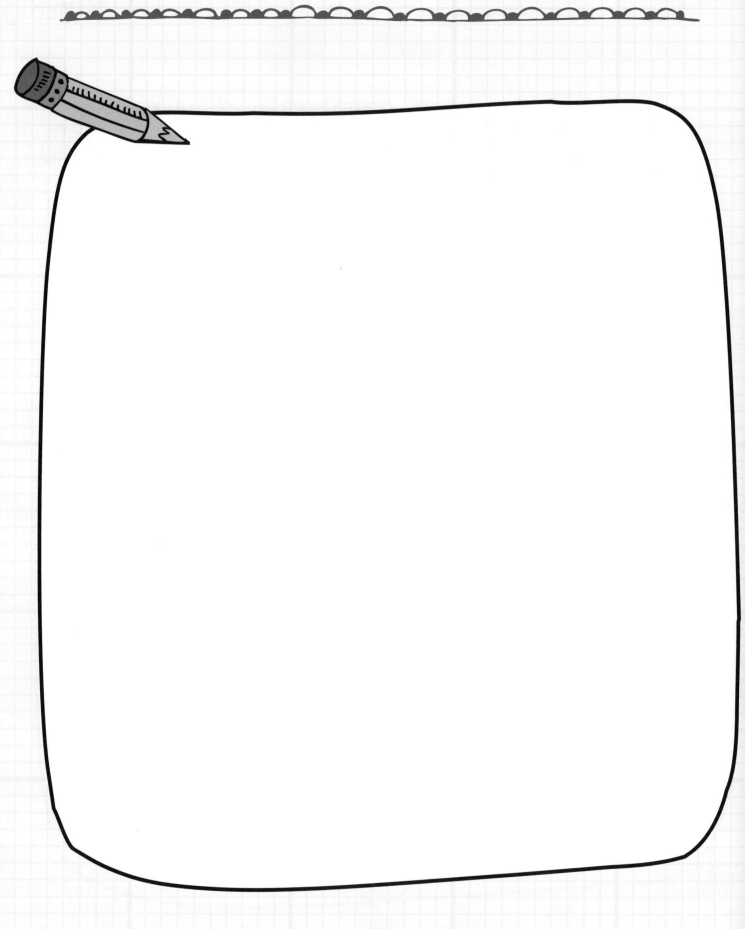

At first, it sounds slightly bonkers to say that there are **only seven basic stories in the world**. There are millions of books and stories out there, how can they all fit into just a handful of plots? But think back to the stories you've come across recently – it's very unlikely you'll come up with one which doesn't fit one (or more) of these plots.

A quick word about genre

Story types are also called **genre**. It's these categories that everyone is familiar with, things like **science fiction, crime, romantic comedy, horror, western** and so on. Stories fit into a genre if they contain at least some of the elements most closely associated with that genre. So, for example, a crime story would usually include some sort of detective and a problem that needs solving. Not all stories fit into a particular genre, and some stories will fit into more than one genre, but these kinds of labels are useful when you want to have a rough idea of what sort of story you're going to get before you begin reading or writing it.

Try something different

If you fancy a change from straightforward text, or 'prose' as it's properly called, you could have a go at writing a story designed to be performed instead of read. Professional play scripts and film scripts have to stick to extremely strict rules about how they're set out on the page. You don't need to worry too much about these but you do need to change the way you write the story down. A play or film script is a set of actions, or directions, rather than a continuous narrative.

For example, in a book you might say:

Tom and Sarah met at Harry's house. Harry's living room was awash with the morning sunlight, which streamed through the window. They sat on the sofa, waiting for Harry to arrive.

"Where is he?" asked Tom crossly. "He said he'd be here."

"Perhaps he's gone to the corner shop," shrugged Sarah.

Tom stalked over to the window and glared out. "I can't see him."

"He's probably upstairs feeding that pet alligator of his," said Sarah. "He loves that reptile."

Angrily, Tom marched out of the room and up the stairs.

FLUFFY

In a script, you need to express the same thing as a series
of instructions:

SCENE: Harry's living room. It is morning.
Light streams through a window. There is a
sofa.

Enter TOM and SARAH. They sit. There is a
pause.

TOM: Where is he? He said he'd be here.

SARAH: Perhaps he's gone to the corner shop.

TOM crosses to the window and looks out.

TOM: I can't see him.

SARAH: He's
probably upstairs
feeding that pet
alligator of his.
He loves
that
reptile.

TOM exits.
We hear
footsteps
ascending
stairs.

ACTIVITY Try writing a short scene of your own!

Presenting your work to an audience

Many writers don't feel confident reading their work out loud to others, but there's no need to feel nervous. An audience wants to hear **what you've got to say.** That's why you're standing up, and they're sitting down listening!

To present your story well, here are a few simple **tricks** and **techniques** that might help you.

1 Speak clearly

Your audience can't enjoy your story if they can't hear it. You don't need to shout, but you do need to **project your voice** well. **Speaking slightly slower** than you normally would will also help your words sound clear.

2 Look up

Even a few **quick glances** up at your audience while you're speaking can help you project your voice and keep the audience focussed on what you're saying. If you feel nervous, one trick is to **look up** but not look at people's faces. Sometimes, eye contact can be distracting!

3 Prepare your script

Write or print your story out with the words a **bit larger** than normal. This will help you keep track of where you are in the story as you speak. If you're reading from a book, or something which can't be enlarged, one trick is to mark a few lines with a highlighter (if that's allowed!), or place strips of sticky notes at intervals down the page. This gives you **visual markers** to help you keep your place.

4 Rehearse

Practise **reading out loud** beforehand, either on your own or in front of a friend or family member. Think about the tips listed above. Don't worry if it doesn't go well the first time, **keep trying**.

Try speaking out loud in front of a mirror using some of the tips above.

CHAPTER 5
FANTASTIC AUTHOR FACTS

Habits of successful authors

Most famous writers have a **particular place** in which they're comfortable writing, whether it's a **favourite chair** or a **special room**. Many also like to write at a particular time of day, or have a daily writing routine.

★ **Roald Dahl** famously wrote in a small hut at the bottom of his garden.

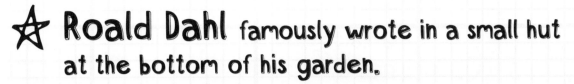

★ Reportedly **Michael Morpurgo** has often written lying down. It's a habit copied from **Robert Louis Stevenson**, author of *Treasure Island*. On the other hand apparently, **Lewis Carroll**, author of *Alice In Wonderland*, used to write standing up. So did **Charles Dickens**.

★ It was reported that **Ian Fleming**, who wrote the James Bond stories, started a new book every January. He'd sit in a corner of his study and type 2000 words every day, until the book was finished.

★ To make sure he finished *The Hunchback Of Notre Dame*, French author **Victor Hugo** apparently locked his clothes away so he couldn't go out. He wore the same knitted shawl for months!

★ Lots of writers base characters on people they know. For example, the fictional detective Sherlock Holmes was based on the real-life Dr Joseph Bell, a tutor at the medical college where Holmes's creator **Sir Arthur Conan Doyle** studied.

ACTIVITY The history of books is jam-packed with **interesting people.** Find out some facts about one of your **favourite authors.**

135

CHAPTER 6
FIND OUT MORE

It's time to **emerge** from your writing den, **blink** a little in the sudden sunlight, and take a **trip** to some of the many book related places there are to visit around the country. For a start, you should keep an eye out for book events near where you live.

There are annual literary **festivals** held all over the place, the biggest being the ones at Bath in Somerset, Cheltenham in Gloucestershire and Hay-On-Wye in Wales. There's likely to be one close enough to you to be worth a day trip. **Bookshops** and **libraries** often hold author readings and book signings. If your local shop hasn't hosted your favourite author recently, contact them and suggest an event.

Here is a list of interesting places you could visit, all linked to the world of books and great writers.

Seven Stories - The National Centre For Children's Books
30 Limee Street, Ouseburn Valley, Newcastle upon Tyne, NE1 2PQ

This features lots of exhibitions and events linked to children's literature past and present.

The Roald Dahl Museum and Story Centre
81-83 High Street, Great Missenden, Buckinghamshire HP16 0AL

The British Library
96 Euston Road, London NW1 2DB

The library contains a vast collection of famous manuscripts, artefacts and book-related treasures.

The Elephant House Tea & Coffee Shop
21 George IV Bridge, Midlothian, Edinburgh EH1 1EN

This is the cafe J.K.Rowling visited a lot when she was writing the first Harry Potter book.

Charles Dickens Museum
48 Doughty Street, London WC1N 2LX

There's also a Charles Dickens Birthplace Museum at 393 Old Commercial Road, Portsmouth PO1 4QL

Sherlock Holmes Museum
221B Baker St, London NW1 6XE

Sherlock Holmes remains one of the most popular fictional characters of all time.

Shakespeare's Birthplace
Henley Street, Stratford-Upon-Avon, Warwickshire
CV37 6QW

This Tudor house gives you an insight into what
life was like in Elizabethan times.

Jane Austen's House Museum
Chawton, Alton, Hampshire GU34 1SD

This is the house where Jane Austen spent
the last eight years of her life.

Last, but definitely
not least:

Your own school library

If ever there was an ideal place
to discover new books, new writers
and new ideas, it's your very own
school library.

MORE
WRITING SPACE